The Healing of the Homosexual

The Healing of the Homosexual

Leanne Payne

Crossway Books • Westchester, Illinois
A Division of Good News Publishers

To all who have endured or even now suffer the homosexual identity crisis, especially those who have feared there is no help to be found. And to all who minister God's healing love to them.

Contents

The Healing of the Homosexual

1: Homosexuality As Identity Crisis

It is in Christ that the complete being of the Godhead dwells embodied, and in him you have been brought to completion. (Colossians 2:9, 10, NEB)

Personality is not a datum from which we start. (C. S. Lewis, "Membership," *The Weight of Glory*)

As a sexual neurosis, homosexuality is regarded as one of the most complex. As a condition for God to heal, it is (in spite of widespread belief to the contrary) remarkably simple. This book is written in the hope that ministers everywhere will take heart and begin to understand how to pray with persons suffering with this problem.

One of the first things to do with the man (or woman) fearing there is no hope or healing for his deep gender confusion is to assure him that there is no such thing, strictly speaking, as a homosexual (or a lesbian). There is only a *person* (an awesome thing to be), created in the image of God, who is cut off from some valid part of himself. God delights in helping us find that lost part, in affirming and blessing it. "The

Son of Man came to seek and to save *what* was lost" (Luke 19:10, italics mine). It is amazing what relief this statement of truth can give to either the one fearing that he or she is homosexual or the one wanting to be delivered from an active homosexual lifestyle.

> When we first *will* to follow—first attempt obedience—God becomes not just some vague force, but very personal. Our idea of Him changes. Then, as He points to the deeps of our personalities, deeps both good and bad that we are not in touch with, our idea about ourselves changes. We find that we do not know ourselves very well. Herein is both the identity crisis and its cure. As we will to be *in Him*, He gathers together the scattered parts of ourselves we have been separated from.
>
> Though this is the key to the healing of us all, this truth is perhaps seen most dramatically in the healing of the homosexual, for his struggle toward wholeness is always associated with deep problems of personal identity. A secure sexual identity is merely part of a secure personal identity—one that spans the full range of what it means to be a human being.[1]

The Cannibal Compulsion
One of the things I often see operating in the homosexual condition, and which illustrates the above, is what I have come to call the "cannibal compulsion." Matthew's story, one of many which I write about in *The Broken Image*, exhibits a classic example of this compulsion. He had sought healing prayer after

achieving a wonderful first success in his chosen career. Rather than rejoicing, however, he began to fall apart.

When Matthew came, breaking under the onslaught of homosexual temptations and dreams, he had no idea of what lay behind them. He could only think of himself as the basest of sinners. How could he, as a Christian, be under such an irrational, powerful, and immoral compulsion? Before we could get into this aspect of his problem, Matthew needed a great deal of prayer for healing of his memories of rejection. He needed to forgive, to be forgiven, and to be released from the effects of his reactions to the sins of others. He needed help in sorting out wrong-headed ideas about God, himself, and others.

By the second session we were ready to deal with the homosexual compulsion, and he was greatly surprised by the following set of questions. In regard to the young man for whom he was experiencing strong homosexual desires I asked him, "What specifically do you admire in this person?" He replied, "His looks, his intellect, the fact that he is successful." These, of course, *were outstanding traits of himself,* but traits that because he could not as yet accept himself, he was denying. I then asked him, "What do you do in your fantasies?" "In my fantasies I want to embrace him, to kiss him on the mouth. I want to come together with him. And in my dreams, that is what I do." After this reply I asked him, "Do you know anything at all about the habits of cannibals? Do you know *why* they eat people?" In utter astonishment he replied, "No, I've no idea why they eat other people." This is a set of questions that are often key in bringing home to such minds and hearts as Matthew's what is really happening in homosexual compulsions. I then told him what a missionary once told me: "Cannibals eat only those they admire, and they eat them *to get their traits.*" What was happening to Matthew was very clear: *he was looking at the other young man and loving a lost part of himself, a part that he could not recognize and accept.*

The first session we'd had together and the resulting prayer for healing of Matthew's painful memories had given me clear insights into both the deprivations he had suffered and the need he had to accept himself. The way was thus paved for this key insight. The strangely idealized vision he had of the young man became increasingly clear. His deep heart knew about this projection, and was revealing the truth in dreams. His "homosexual" dreams that were so frightening to him when taken literally were in effect good messengers sent to say, "Look, you are trying to integrate with a lost part of yourself, but you are going about it the wrong way."

The compelling force behind Matthew's homosexual compulsions was the fact that he was painfully estranged from parts of himself. And several of these parts, consisting of *unaffirmed* and therefore unintegrated attributes of his personality, had played no small part in the professional and artistic success he had just scored. In waking life and in the dream, the young man whom he so ardently admired symbolized these attributes and capabilities of his own personality. Therefore, the way in which we were to pray was at once clear and simple. We would pray specifically that Matthew might be able to recognize, accept, and *come together with* that part of himself he was projecting onto the other young man: the handsome, intellectually keen, and successful Matthew that had never been affirmed by his parents. As we prayed, we would visualize this happening and thus release our faith into a powerful prayer of faith. This one healing prayer would then immediately defuse the power behind the homosexual compulsion.

The Prayer
Once Matthew had gotten a fair understanding of what had been going on inside himself, he was ready and eager for prayer that he might accept those attributes of his own personality he had been projecting onto another. This prayer, as the following weeks proved, did indeed rob the homosexual compulsions of their sting and power.

His immediate need, that of acknowledging those traits vital to his recent success, now identified and ministered to, could no longer plague him by masquerading as a homosexual compulsion. This, however, was only the beginning step in the much larger healing he needed—that of enablement to fully accept himself. He had not known affirmation of himself as a *person*, as a *man*, as a *being of worth*. Within himself were these unaffirmed identities. It was too late for his father and mother to affirm him in a deeply healing and meaningful way, much less for someone else (like myself perhaps) to try to substitute for them. At this point he didn't need a mother or father—he needed to *face the inner loneliness with God*. His full healing would come as he learned to wait, listening, in the Presence of God. In this two-way conversation between himself and God, his full affirmation would come. My part was to invoke the Presence, to call him into it, to see always the real Matthew and appeal only to the man God was calling forth.[2]

We see the "cannibal compulsion" again in Stan's story:

Stan's dilemma was chiefly due to the smallness of his person. Because of his anguish over this, he had doubts and fears about his sexual capabilities. These anxieties grew as he continued to reject his small body, and with it his own masculinity. As a college senior and long past the period of puberty, he had as yet failed to accept himself and go on from there to gain a secure sexual identity. This problem became critical when he, like Matthew, found himself enmeshed by compulsive homosexual fantasies.

These started with unbidden mental images which assaulted his mind when he would see other fellows in gym showers. Invariably these images would concern the athletic types. Stan, unlike Matthew, did not admire the intellect and the good looks of another, but the physical size and athletic prowess that characterizes the All-American athlete. To his current state of mind, these were the characteristics essential to sexual virility. The unbidden imagery darting in and out of Stan's mind therefore centered on the genitals of the male he admired. And here again we recognize the analogy between the homosexual compulsion and the cannibal's reason for eating a fellow human—in order to get his good traits. Both reflect a twisted way we try to take into ourselves those attributes we feel we are missing.

An unbidden and recurring mental image that suddenly assails the mind, when it is *entertained subjectively,* becomes part of an ongoing compulsive fantasy in that person's life. On the other hand, when it is immediately *objectified*— that is, held outside oneself (so to speak) and analyzed—one not only can begin to read its psychological implications, but take authority over it. Whether it is a symbolic picture welling up from an unhealed psyche, or a destructive missile from the enemy of our souls, it can be discerned through prayer and thereby utterly disarmed. Often it is both these things working together, and we must take care to pray for the healing of the psychological factor as well as that of the spiritual. In this way we discern between the need for healing the soul and its protection and deliverance from the alien forces that would oppress and lie to it. Satan, both tempter and accuser (Revelation 12:10), takes full advantage of a person's psychological problem (in Stan's case, his failure to secure his sexual identity).

Stan lost the battle in this onslaught against the mind by allowing lust to enter in. More than a little influenced by the current homosexual propaganda and having failed to secure his sexual identity, he began subjectively to entertain, rather than objectify and take authority over, the phallic images that plagued his mind. In this way he opened himself to temptation and, finally, to a moral and spiritual fall that ended in overt homosexual acts.

Had Stan gotten the help he needed before falling into overt homosexual behavior, he would have spared himself intense suffering, for he very quickly came under severe demonic oppression. He had always been a very sensitive, moral person, and had won honors for academic and artistic excellence in a university noted for both. His mind, however, was now held captive not only by a demonic imagery, but by a vicious and continuous mental obsession that contained two elements: a constant analyzing of himself, an exercise in which he was continually looking inward to find some sort of a personal truth or reality, and a constant analyzing of what he had before accepted as true. This inner dialogue was full of an irrational sophistry that could only tear concepts apart, but could never put the fragments back together in any kind of satisfying whole. Another way to describe this is to say that his thought, severely introspective and full of doubts about what is or is not true, was agonizingly painful and circular. This is the disease of introspection, and Stan had it to a fearful degree. He was in fact floundering in serious mental and spiritual darkness and was filled with fear when he first sought help through prayer.

Our first prayer was one in which I commanded the powers of darkness to release his mind and depart from him. I use Holy Water (water blessed and prayed over by a priest and set apart for this purpose) in such a prayer so as always to have the prayers of the Church united with mine. It is one of the simplest and quickest prayers we are privileged to pray, and only requires that we know and move in the authority given to us as Christians. The Holy Spirit's gift of discerning of spirits is in operation *before* such a prayer is made. The relief this prayer brings, once the demonic is truly discerned and sent away, is immediate.

The next prayer for Stan was with anointing of oil for the healing and quieting of the mind. Under the Holy Spirit's leading, we pray according to that person's individual need. Usually in a case like this, however, I anoint the forehead with oil, making the sign of the cross on the forehead. Then, laying my hands on the head (or sometimes gently pressing both temples), I ask Jesus to enter in, and to heal and quiet the mind. I wait, quietly praying, *seeing* Him do this very thing. After this prayer, Stan was ready to make his confession and receive the needed cleansing and forgiveness.

After this we had to tackle his psychological need, that of accepting himself as small, and of accepting his masculinity even though it came in a smaller frame than he had heretofore been able to accept. Ideally this step should have been taken just after puberty and long before this time. It was yet a formidable leap for him, and he needed sensitive love, wisdom, and affirmation from one who would wait and listen to the Lord with him until such time as he could make the hurdle safely.

This is, as we have seen, an attitudinal block which we overcome as we deliberately *choose* to forsake our old unaccepting and unloving attitudes toward the self and bring the thoughts of the mind and the imaginations of the heart (in this case, all the old negative thoughts and imaginations about oneself) into subjection to Christ (2 Corinthians 10:5). We then begin to see ourselves, not through our own eyes or even the eyes of others, but through His loving, accepting eyes. We are thus instilled with, and learn to exercise, the virtue of patience and gentleness toward ourselves as well as others. It is on our knees—or however we best get into a two-way conversation with God—that we consciously and deliberately accept ourselves, and begin the task of *listening,* of becoming present to our own hearts as well as to the heart of God.

Particularly humiliating memories from the past can make us afraid to listen to God and to our own inner selves and feelings, for fear of what we might find when we do. Some of us fear that when we really face the truth about ourselves, we will know for sure that our worst fears are in fact true—that we are somehow viler than others, or perhaps less "normal" than everyone else we know. We run then from facing our inner loneliness and are terrified of either solitude on the one hand, or of the satisfying intimacy and companionship we need with our friends and family on the other. But all who take their courage in hand and enter into this kind of prayer, no longer fearing to see and acknowledge before Him either the ignoble things in their past or their deep inner feelings about themselves *and others,* are the ones who find that God is truly love. They also find the virtue (a gift from God) of self-acceptance.

For Stan, even after he had accepted God's forgiveness, the *fact* that he *had fallen* in such a way held him back from accepting himself and therefore from the goal of freedom and maturity. Besides forgiving himself, he had to be patient and gentle toward the self that had erred, and reject only the sinful behavior. Stan had to realize that a failure to do this could only be rooted in pride.

This is the pride that until realized and confessed bars us from coming to terms with the fact that we are, like everyone else, fallen creatures, and therefore are sinful and do make grievous mistakes. This failure is usually hiding under what we term an "inferiority complex," something that always involves a form of pride lurking within. We are yet trying to work out our own salvation. In confessing our pride, we acknowledge that we are like all other men—fallen and prone to the vile as well as to the beautiful, and that if we turn from Him but for a moment we are once again capable of the shameful and the sordid. This is the full acceptance of the way of the cross—God's way of saving us which bypasses our attempts to win salvation for having been perfect, or having figured out a way to "undo" our past sins and mistakes.

Usually, once this great truth of free and "amazing grace" is understood, a person can go on to settle the matter of self-acceptance by himself. This ordinarily takes a good bit of "wrestling" in prayer against our old attitudes, but that is what makes us strong. In cases where the diseased emotional view toward the self is particularly difficult and of long standing, however, more help is needed. With these persons, my part is simply to wait with them in prayer, gently directing them to let go of their negative ideas, and receive in their place the positive words and attitudes the Lord sends. Sometimes, in particularly difficult cases, we go back into the memories that have already been healed through prayer. This time, however, the person is consciously and deliberately, in conversation with the Lord, to *accept* the self who has participated in the hated behavior and take care to reject only the harmful behavior.

In this way, those who are so rejecting of themselves can gain the necessary objectivity they need to exercise the same patient acceptance of themselves as they would toward another person. This is, at the same time, a deeply meaningful lesson in a proper humility, the kind that humbly accepts the penitent and forgiven self. It frees those like Stan from the depression their anger toward themselves has generated. This kind of prayer defuses, deflects, and indeed entirely disperses the anger. Thus humbled before Him, they are enabled to accept themselves, and He lifts them up and makes their lives meaningful.

This listening prayer is the best possible training in the practice of the Presence of God. In looking to Him, we are drawn up and out of the hell of self-consciousness and introspection. We become God-conscious. Stan learned resolutely to check himself when he was turning inward—the practice of the presence of self—and, in that very moment, to cast his mind and the eyes of his heart (imagination) on the Lord. "I will keep him in perfect peace whose mind is stayed on Me" (Isaiah 26:3) has always been the promise of God, and it is the very best way of all to be healed of the disease of introspection.

In this *listening prayer* new light is shed on one's past, and we gather insight into the *whys* of our particular weaknesses. Stan, himself a perfectionist, began to realize that in this he reflected his father's perfectionism. Along with this, he saw that two basic attitudinal patterns had evolved in himself: (1) the pattern of not wanting to displease, and (2) the pattern of being subservient to his mother through fear of displeasing her. He saw that he had tried to protect his mother in this way, and why he had done so. His brother, a year or so older, had been unmanageable, and his mother, attributing this to the fact of his sex, prayed and prayed that the next baby would be a girl. Instead of the girl, Stan arrived, and he somehow realized his mother's fear of having another difficult son. From as far back as he could remember, he tried to be perfect. He tried to fulfill all her expectations as to what a good baby and a good son would be. In later deference to her, he did not attempt to establish the usual boy-girl relationships. All this came as new insight to Stan and was the fruit of his exchanging the old habit of introspection for the discipline of listening prayer.

These personal circumstances, of course, did not prepare him for the work of separating his identity (sexual and otherwise) from that of his mother, but there was an even more important factor in this difficulty. His father, though a very fine man, was deeply engrossed in his work and was also emotionally remote from his son. Stan, an intensely loyal person, could hardly admit that he barely knew his father, though he had placed him high on a pedestal. He therefore did not have the necessary relationship with his father during the crucial years of puberty and immediately after, that time when he so desperately needed paternal affirmation in order to emerge from the narcissistic cocoon of adolescence and accept his mature masculine identity.

To listen is to obey. In learning obedience, one's true self—masculinity and all—comes forward. As Stan made his will one with Christ's he found and accepted his full masculine identity. It was there all the time—waiting for him. He did not win it without a struggle, but in the struggle was the full metamorphosis. Like the butterfly moth, he grew very strong and brightly colored wings with which to fly and explore the universe. He is a sturdy stable person now, one who is amiable, content, and in possession of his heterosexual identity. His academic and artistic talents have blossomed and at the time of this writing are earning him extraordinary success.

I believe one of the strong demonic intentions was to bereave him of his unusually fine artistic and intellectual talent. Another factor bears mentioning, one that left him all the more open to such a serious assult on his mind. In lieu of having accepted himself, Stan totally immersed himself in intellectual and artistic pursuits, and neglected the spiritual, physical, and emotional parts of his being. We are more vulnerable to temptations and odd compulsions when we develop one part of the mind or personality at the expense of another.[3]

2: The World's, the Church's, and the Scriptural Views of Homosexuality

The *world's* current view of homosexuality consists mainly of the notion that (1) one's "sexual preference" is determined genetically and there is essentially nothing one can do about it, one must simply accept it; or (2) homosexuality is an alternate lifestyle that ought to be explored and enjoyed—there is nothing wrong with it, we have simply been prejudiced against it.

The *Church's* current view seems mainly to be that (1) the homosexual sufferer must grin and bear his problem, just live with it while remaining chaste and celibate; or (2) the homosexual lifestyle should be, as in the view of Virginia Mollenkott, Letha Scanzoni, and others, lovingly accepted and perhaps even blessed by the Church.[4]

Finally and happily, there is the *scriptural* view that homosexuality is something to be repented of and healed: "That is what some of you were" (1 Corinthians 6:11). The sinful aspect has to do with the lameness of the human spirit and is healed through confession and absolution of personal sin. The psychological aspect is part of the lameness of the soul, that which is to be set straight so that both spirit and soul can grow into freedom. A wounded person needs healing as well as pardon.

The Ministry of Healing

Under the anointing of the Holy Spirit and in the power and authority of Christ's Name, we are to preach, teach, and heal. We have been more or less faithful to the preaching and teaching, but have not always understood how to pray for healing of the souls entrusted to us.

All healing has to do with mended relationships. Christ commanded and empowered His followers to heal, because He knew that all men, in their exterior relationships and *within* themselves, are broken and separated. In order for man to regain wholeness in every aspect of his life, the relationship between himself and God, himself and other men, himself and nature, and himself and his innermost being must be healed. The fallen condition is a crisis in separation, and within the trauma of broken relationships resides what is aptly described as the identity crisis. It is through prayer that relationships are mended and that our souls are healed of their grievous lacks due to failed relationships in the past.

> Jesus went round all the towns and villages teaching in their synagogues, announcing the good news of the Kingdom, and curing every kind of ailment and disease. The sight of the people moved him to pity: they were like sheep without a shepherd, harrassed and helpless; and he said to his disciples, 'The crop is heavy, but labourers are scarce; you must therefore beg the owner to send labourers to harvest his crop.' Then he called his twelve disciples to him and gave them authority to cast out unclean spirits and to cure every kind of ailment and disease. (Matthew 9:35—10:1, NEB)

Oswald Chambers, commenting on this Scripture in *My Utmost for His Highest*, says,

> The key is prayer, not work, that is, not work as the word is popularly understood today. . . . He (the Lord) owns the harvest that is produced by distress and conviction of sin, and this is the harvest we have to pray that labourers may be thrust out to reap. We are taken up with active work while people all round are ripe to harvest, and we do not reap one of them, but waste our Lord's time in overenergized activities.[5]

Here Oswald Chambers is putting his finger squarely on what is meant by prayer for healing of the soul (healing of memories or inner healing), and on the fact that we are not doing it. Healing of memories means forgiveness of sin, and any teaching on prayer for the healing of the soul's woundedness that is separated from that scriptural doctrine in any way is misguided and misleading. (There are those who secularize this teaching and separate the two.) The healing of memories is the forgiveness of sin applied at the level for which it was intended, that of the deep heart (the unconscious mind). Agnes Sanford coined the term at a time when very little healing was flowing through the Church's formal confessional or in informal prayer groups, and this was because the central truth of God's forgiveness of sin, along with all the great spiritual realities of the Kingdom of God, had been largely relegated to the abstract. We ministers had gotten very "heady." We could talk a blue streak about forgiveness, but we couldn't administer it to the heart in need of it. We could not, in other words, reap the "harvest that is produced by distress and conviction of sin," whether sin on the part of the one we prayed for or sin on the part of those who wounded him.

> And the people all tried to touch him, because power was coming from him and healing them all. (Luke 6:19)

This concept of the power to heal was missing. We could perhaps see it in Christ two millennia ago, but could not, for the life of us or of the world, see how that applied to us. As twentieth-century ministers and doctors, our heads were filled with the psychologies of the day, to the exclusion of the understanding of the power of God that can and must flow through us, *incarnationally,* to the sick and penitent. Agnes Sanford, like Oswald Chambers, knew this, and she coined the term "healing of memories" in order to help us remove the doctrine of the forgiveness of sin from an abstract realm, and rightly connect it to our responsibility to heal the wounds sin leaves in the soul.

> The truth is that any wound to the soul so deep that it is not healed by our own self-searching and prayers is inevitably connected with a sub-conscious awareness of sin, either our own sins or our grievous reactions to the sins of others.
> The therapy that heals these deep wounds could be called the forgiveness of sins or it could be called the healing of memories. Whatever one calls it, there are in many of us wounds so deep that only the mediation of someone else to whom we may "bare our grief" can heal us."[6]

King David understood this healing very well:

> I acknowledged my sin to you, and my iniquity I did not hide. I said I will confess my transgressions to the Lord (continually unfolding the past till all is told); then You (instantly) forgave me the guilt and iniquity of my sin. (Psalm 32:5, *Amplified*)

In prayer for healing of memories, we not only confess our sin, but we forgive those people and circumstances that have so wounded and grieved us. Sometimes the memories where forgiveness is needed go back before we can consciously remember, and here, most dramatically of all perhaps, we see come into play the gifts of healing that God has entrusted to the Church. It is no small thing, for example, to see a person healed who has been hospitalized, perhaps several times, due to rejections they experienced *before* birth. Vivid in my mind is the intrauterine memory God healed within the deep mind and heart of a young woman who had twice been hospitalized with depression after having abused her young children. It took three other ministers, along with myself, to hold her down as she relived the memory of her mother's attempt to abort her with a sharp instrument. In inviting God into her memories, in asking Him to find the root behind her mental illness, in her forgiving her mother, and in our binding through prayer the effects of that sin against her, she found wholeness. She is a stable, well-balanced wife and mother this very day, some ten years after forgiveness took place.

The "unconscious" mind, that extensive area of the psyche (soul) that is not in the immediate field of awareness, houses the memory bank. It never forgets. There sorrowful, shameful memories are suppressed. They do not disappear, and need healing through forgiveness.

> We have a strange illusion that mere time cancels sins. I have heard others, and I have heard myself, recounting cruelties and falsehoods committed in boyhood as if they were no concern of the present speaker's, and even with laughter. But mere time does nothing either to the fact or to the guilt of sin. The guilt is washed out not by time but by repentance and the blood of Christ.[7]

Time does not wipe out sin. For this reason, when a church, a nation, or an individual repents, incredible things happen. New life floods in. When we learn to pray for healing of the wounds of sin (we are all wounded, having been born into a fallen world), then psychological miracles occur.

Christ collaborated with the Spirit to do His work of healing and teaching (see Luke 5:17; Acts 1:2), and so do we. The gift of healing is a ministry of the Holy Spirit and never the precocious effort of an individual. Therefore, the first step I take with the man or woman in need of healing is *to invoke the Presence of the Lord and invite that one into the healing Presence.* There we listen together for the healing word our Lord is always sending. (See *The Broken Image,* Chapter 6, "Listening for the Healing Word.")

How We Lost the Ability to Listen

As Christians, we lost the understanding of how to heal the soul because we lost, to a very great extent, the Judeo-Christian understanding of the heart (that is, the deep mind and its way of knowing or spiritually perceiving). This mind, which we often foggily think of as the "unconscious," is the intuitive rather than the reasoning faculty. It is the seat of the creative imagination, the memory, and the gifts of the Holy Spirit—all so vital to the ministry of prayer for healing of the soul. We can trace this loss of understanding to

our inheritance of Greek thought, particularly from Aristotle. Aristotle's epistemology confined man's ways of receiving knowledge to the data received through his sense experience and his reason. By synthesizing experience, reason was thought capable of putting man in touch with the real. From these two ways of knowing (experience and reason), both belonging to the conscious mind, he developed his first principles of knowledge. He thus ruled out Plato's third way of knowing, which included the ways of divine inspiration, of the poet and the prophet, of the dream and of the vision, and—most important of all—the way of love. These of course are the ways of the "unconscious" mind: the way of picture, metaphor, symbol, myth, and—with love— the way of Incarnation: that way which brings myth and fact together. Had this way of knowing been retained, we no doubt would not have the somewhat self-contradictory term "unconscious mind" in our vocabulary today, since this way is really not unconscious at all, but involves several different sorts of consciousness.

As the Church, principally through St. Thomas Aquinas, came to accept the Aristotelian epistemology and incorporate it into its theology, the Judeo-Christian understanding of the deep heart (the unconscious mind and its ways of knowing) simply dropped from sight. There were no categories by which to recognize it. Christians and non-Christians alike came to value exclusively the conscious mind and its ways of knowing over those of the unconscious. This has not only greatly hampered the Western Christian's understanding of the creative imagination, but it has mightily suppressed our understanding of the work of the Holy Spirit in man. Indeed, the development and integration of the whole man in his relationship to God, to other men, and to those things within himself have not been fully understood because of our failure to understand our two minds.[8]

Our two minds, the intellect and the heart, stand in antithesis. Opposite and complementary one to the other, they do not work in ways at all comparable. They are the analytical masculine mind as over against the feminine intuitive mind, science as over against wisdom, scientific statement as over against poetic statement. This is the discovery that C. S. Lewis says "flashed a new light back on my whole life,"[9] and this discovery is vital to all who would minister in the power of the Holy Spirit. To lose the good of one mind is eventually to lose the good of the other as well. We in the Church, for example, often lose the good of reason because we are unable to see and hear God with the eyes and ears of our hearts.[10]

3: Barriers to Inner Healing

The three major barriers to inner healing (failure to forgive others, failure to receive forgiveness for ourselves, and failure to accept ourselves) are illustrated in Matthew's and Stan's stories. The first two barriers were largely removed for them in prayer for the healing of memories during our first session together. The healing of the traumatic rejections they had suffered had to begin first, because these old wounds were behind their failures to accept themselves. They found, as we all do of course, that as more illumination is given, there is more to forgive and for which to be forgiven. Matthew's release, after the initial healing prayers,

> was such a soaring and joyful thing that at first he thought he had no further need. But this was the basic healing that would enable him to look upward freely and begin the breathtaking uphill climb from immaturity (freedom from his old inner vision of himself) to maturity with its proper humility and self-acceptance, which is the antithesis to self-centeredness, the wrong kind of self-consciousness and self-love. With this healing he could press on into the freedom

to act from the center of his being, that center where Christ dwells and forms the new man, rather than from the locus of the unloved and hurting little boy under the authority of unloving parents and an enigmatic world.

The leveling of this third barrier would require some time, for on the one hand it entailed changing the attitudes and thought-habits of a lifetime. Fr. Michael Scanlon, in his fine book entitled *Inner Healing*, states it this way: "We have an attitudinal life which operates from the very core of our being. . . . This life determines broad general patterns of relating to others and to God." And just as importantly, I would add, *to ourselves*. This is because we cannot love God and others while hating ourselves, while failing to exercise patience and charity toward ourselves. Of this great virtue of patience with the self, the Catholic philosopher Romano Guardini has said, "He who wishes to advance must always begin again. . . . Patience with oneself . . . this is the foundation of all progress."

On the other hand, it entails the "putting on" of Christ and the taking up of the new life. In so doing, every thought of the mind and every picture of the heart is brought into subjection to Christ—a real "practice of the Presence." This is no exercise in abstraction, or even of positive thinking (though it is that and more), but a waiting on Him who is within, without, and all around us, the utter Reality who is capable at any moment of manifesting Himself to the creatures He has fashioned in His own image. Thus we are "made new in mind and spirit, and put on the new nature of God's creating."

Having put Him on, we know that Another is Lord, Another is in charge. Having received Him into ourselves, we know that Another lives through us. The fruits of His indwelling Presence ("love, joy, peace, patience, kindness, goodness, fidelity, gentleness, and self-control," Galatians 5:22, 23, NEB) now issue through us to others, and we who are the channels are healed as well as others in their fragrant wholesome atmosphere. The gifts of this Presence—the power to know, to say, to act—is ours, and we become the masterpiece of harmony God intended us to be. The work of our hands is affirmed. In union and communion with Him, our once fragmented souls are drawn together in one harmonious whole even as the pieces of a complex puzzle fall in place under the guidance of a masterful hand. We are no longer divided within. The psalmist is praying for this healing, I believe, when he cries unto the Lord, "*Unite* my heart to fear thy Name" (Psalm 86:11).

The Presence calls forth the true self, up and out of the hell of the false old self, in what can best be described as a resurrection. The true self, with one face, no longer repressed, fearful, or unsteady, shakes off the old pseudo-selves with their myriad faces, and comes boldly forward, gathering all that is valid and real in the personality into itself. We are united within. It is then we can realize the freedom to live out from that center of our being, that place where His Spirit indwells ours, and our will is one with Him. We begin to practice not only His presence, but the presence of the new man. We are free from practicing the presence of the old man in whom the principle of death and evil holds sway, and also that of the immature man who is yet under a law (see Galatians 4).

As Matthew well knew, we can be Christians and remain under the law—utterly fail to realize our inheritance and our capacity to walk in the Spirit and practice the presence of the new man. Rather, we practice the presence of the guilty little boy or girl, the "unable to receive the love of God or man" little boy or girl, and are thus rendered unable to exercise the mature authority needed over our own lives or in positions of leadership in the Body of Christ. For this reason too, we cannot move strongly and effectively in the healing gifts of the Spirit. False humility, actual sin, or need for psychological healing bars us from living out from the center, a position of knowing who we are in Him. This position is one of authority, and one by which we the redeemed, even as the unfallen Adam, are *namers* of all that is created. Named by God, and molded by His will alone, we are no longer named and shaped by that which is created. This is the maturity and authority that heals the world. We die daily to any selfish or tyrannical authority (a carnal, dominating spirit) that comes from living out of the self-centered old man, as well as to the weak position of "no authority" of the minor under a law; we live from the center, where He dwells, naming in His name. Our true masculinity is restored. This all creation waits for. All this is involved in the tearing down of the third barrier and of coming into our true identity. It does not happen overnight.

Yet such a healing as this can and does take place so much more quickly than is ordinarily supposed. Often, in contrast to the years of counseling sessions many regularly undergo, two or three weeks will see this healing well underway, depending upon how willing the person is to set aside his own will and learn how to listen to God. Listening prayer is the way to a quick leveling of this third barrier to inner healing. This is a type of prayer all should practice, but often we must be brought to the utterly helpless position of a Matthew before we will give over our servitude to all the other voices within and without and begin to hear and obey the voice of the Good Shepherd. Many of these persons—having suffered breakdowns and long hospitalizations in the past—end up being the strongest and most effective Christians because, having been under such bondage to the voices of the past and present, they gladly *listen* for the life-giving Word in order to survive as persons.

More About the Failure to Accept Ourselves

Within this third barrier to inner healing lies a failure to negotiate what is at one level a perfectly natural developmental step common to all men everywhere. There are, as the psychologists point out, progressions from infancy to maturity which involve steps of "psycho-social development." When we miss one of these normal progressions, we are in trouble.

One of the progressions vital to this matter of self-acceptance is the step *from* the narcissistic period of puberty, that "auto-erotic," self-centered phase when one's attention is more or less painfully centered on one's own body and self, *to* that developmental level whereby one has accepted himself and has turned his eyes and heart outward toward all else in the created world. To whatever degree one fails in regard to this step, he will find himself stuck in some form or manifestation of the wrong kind of self-love. Failing to love himself aright, he will love himself amiss. The rampant morbid practice of introspection, for example, is one of the most prevalent of these manifestations, and the anxious practice of it can be as pernicious to personality development as that of masturbation (when carried past puberty) and homosexuality—two of the more obvious examples of a love turned inward.

There are, of course, a multitude of ways in which we can love the self to the exclusion of others. I remember only too well the young wife who realized her husband's narcissism in his very act of lovemaking. She said to me, "My husband is in love with his own body. I am most aware of this when he is making love to me. He doesn't really—can't really—make love to me, though I can hardly explain it to you. I have seen him nude, gesturing before a mirror. He gets the same pleasure out of that as in making love to me. I am not loved. I am merely a vessel through whom he loves himself." This man sorely needed the healing we are here talking about. In meeting with him later I found that he suffered fits of black depression in which he despised himself. He needed freedom from a narcissistic love the flipside of which was a non-acceptance and even hatred of the self.

To write about the healing of the homosexual is to write about the healing of all men and women, for every one of us has been stuck in some diseased form of self-love. Indeed, that is what the Fall in every individual life *is*. Christ not only redeems us from the effects of the Fall, but continues to free us as we come regularly before Him repenting the pride that continues so quickly and easily to beset us. Always, in order to keep whole, we must continue to confess pride, that root of all darkness, the self-serving kind of love.

Walter Trobisch has written on the need for self-acceptance in a booklet entitled *Love Yourself* (Downers Grove, Ill.: InterVarsity Press, 1978). In it he states simply and truthfully two facts that I see borne out continually in respect to the right kind of self-love. First, "It is an established fact that nobody is born with the ability to love himself" (p. 8). He then quotes the German psychotherapist Dr. Guido Groeger: "Self-love is either acquired or it is nonexistent. The one who does not acquire it or who acquires it insufficiently either is not able to love others at all or to love them only insufficiently. The same would be true for such a person in his relationship to God" (p. 9). Second, Walter Trobisch states: "To put it bluntly, *Whoever does not love himself is an egoist*. He must become an egoist necessarily because he is not sure of his identity and is therefore always trying to find himself. Like Narcissus, being engrossed with himself, he becomes self-centered (p. 15).

"An example of self-love in the negative sense is illustrated by the Greek myth about

Narcissus. He was a youth who, while gazing at his reflection in a well, fell in love with himself. Totally engrossed with his own image, he tumbled into the water and drowned. From this myth, the word *narcissism* is derived. Another Greek term for 'self' and 'love' denoting the same idea is *auto-eroticism*.

"Self-love used in the positive sense of self-acceptance is the exact opposite of narcissism or auto-eroticism. It is actually a prerequisite for a step in the direction of selflessness. We cannot give what we do not possess. Only when we have accepted ourselves can we become truly selfless and free from ourselves. If, however, we have not found ourselves and discovered our own identity, then we must continually search for ourselves. The word *self-centered* aptly describes us when we revolve only around ourselves" (pp. 14, 15).

The failure to pass from the narcissistic stage on into that of self-acceptance is what we are here calling the third barrier to inner healing, the failure to accept and love oneself aright. I have written at some length on this matter because of the fact, greatly impressed on me as I studied the data of each healing, that this failure is common to each one, no matter what category of homosexuality his or her story fits in. A study of homsexuality turns out to be a study of arrested growth in at least a part of the personality; it is a study in immaturity. Indeed, it is a study in both the psychological and spiritual aspects of the identity crisis.

Equally as thought-provoking to me has

been the importance of the father's role during, and in the formative years just after, puberty. It appears to be crucial to the young son or daughter's negotiation of this "psycho-social developmental step." The father's affirmation of his young one has been indispensable all along, of course, laying as it does the groundwork for a trusting relationship later on. But he must not opt out at this critical time in the life of the adolescent. The fact that the father's loving and affirming presence (or that of an extraordinary father substitute) is the ladder by which the young son or daughter takes this crucial developmental step up to self-acceptance has been impressed on me over and over again. This calls for a reasonably whole father, one who has himself made the step. His part is then the crucial one, even as the mother's was during the first months of life, from conception to the child's realization that it is a separate entity from her. There is never a time in a child's life when it does not need the love of a whole father and a whole mother, but apparently some stages are more critical than others for psychological health and development.

It is one of the tragedies of our culture that fewer and fewer of us move from puberty on into this step. We remain in various arrested states below that of a serene self-acceptance, with its release from the mood swings between a selfish egoism on the one hand and an annihilating self-hatred on the other. Thus we are slaves to our own emotional beings, and we live precariously out from the locus of our own feeling beings. This we do until the pain of having missed this developmental step grows so intense that we begin to awaken from our stupor, and begin the search for wholeness. Many, never finding answers and healing, go to their graves never having stepped across the line from immaturity to maturity. The main reasons for this cultural impasse are not hard to find. The father is simply more often than not unavailable to his adolescent son or daughter. This may be by reason of divorce or simply because no time is left over from business or profession. Often the father's own self-serving manner of life and immaturity render him unable to affirm his son or daughter. Or it may even be that our permissive society has prematurely freed the son or daughter from the father's rightful authority. Much of the homosexuality we see today is the harvest sown by the breakup of the American home and the absence of whole and affirming fathers.[11]

4: Gender Identity

From our Lord's ministry, we can see that no two healings are ever the same, and therefore prayers for healing can never be reduced to mere formulas or methods. But in prayers with persons who fear that they may be homosexual, and with those involved in homosexual behavior—whether overt or in the fantasy life—I've come to recognize certain root problems and basic psychological needs. As I point out in *The Broken Image*, these fall into discernible groups. But they could all be written about from the standpoint of gender imbalance. Both Matthew and Stan, for example, were alienated from their masculine side. Both, unaffirmed *as men* by their fathers, needed specific prayer for the separation of their sexual identity from that of their mothers, and for the grace to accept their own. A man, unaffirmed in his masculinity, can fully integrate with it as he learns to come into the Presence of God the Father, the Master Affirmer. There, listening to Him, he begins to "taste," as it were, the divine Masculine that resurrects his own.

I have written an entire book, *Crisis in Masculinity* (Crossway Books, 1985), on the kind of prayer needed for this healing because, tragically, we live in a day when the unaffirmed male is the rule rather than the exception. I pray with—and see the healing of—men who are almost totally severed from their masculine identities. Gender identity is an awesome thing to write about, for it is a vital part of the true self and, as such, has spiritual (utterly transcendent), as well as psychological, dimensions. The following story illustrates the pain of gender imbalance in a woman:

Recently I met for healing prayer with Judy, a handsome young woman whose need to forgive her mother was repressed and denied. This emotional turmoil lay at an "unconscious" level of her mind and heart and had to be brought to her awareness before she could be freed from the wrong kind of ties to her mother. It also had to happen before she could be released from strong and abnormal compulsions she was all too keenly conscious of: those accompanying a severe symbolic gender confusion, the lesbian neurosis.

Judy, as her friends call her, is successful in what historically has been a male profession, and in her the conscious analytical masculine mind is highly developed. She climbs mountains with the most gifted male climbers, and has developed her physical powers to the utmost. In these and in other ways the drive toward power which is common to the male is demonstrated in her. In short, she is gifted with the masculine *power to initiate* to a high degree. All this is fine for the woman who is fully in touch with her feminine side, but Judy was not; she was out of balance. She was not in touch with her inner self (the feminine intuitive mind) enough to realize she needed to forgive her mother, and she was severely separated from what turned out to be a very beautiful *woman* within.

She had a history of lesbian activity behind her, and certain women continued to "spark" her, she said. Her need for intimacy was great, and she was, at age thirty-one, utterly unfree to relate to men. "Do I have to live and die with this thing never taken care of in me?" she cried.

The gender drive in a woman is the drive to respond to and receive the male. Biologically, physically, psychologically, unless this is stymied, it is natural to woman. She can make herself at home in the inner world of the man she loves. Elisabeth Elliot, in line with the best wisdom of the ages, captures this truth when she states, "The essence of masculinity is initiation and the essence of feminity is response." Judy had never known this drive.

I assured Judy that she certainly did not have to live and die without this thing taken care of in her, that there was no such thing, strictly speaking, as a lesbian or homosexual, that she was simply alienated from some valid part of herself. And I assured her that God would help us find it that very day. I then asked her what story in *The Broken Image* particularly spoke to her. Here is where "not being in touch with our own inner self enough to know we haven't forgiven" comes in: she felt she did not quite fit any of the "lesbian cases" she had read about in *The Broken Image*. As it turned out, hers was a classic example of one category written about in the book, the one where lesbian behavior is connected to a woman's need to be set free from the effects of having an extremely possessive and dominating mother (see pages 102-106).

Judy's mother was in her late forties when Judy, an only child, was born. When I asked her how her mother was as a feminine role model, she quickly replied, "Oh, I don't think of my mother as a woman." At those words, I realized Judy had rejected the femininity of her mother and in doing so, had somehow rejected her own.

In cases of homosexuality, the rejection of a parent often needs to be confessed and renounced before the person can find wholeness. I find this to be the case time and again in both men and women. For a young lad to seriously reject his own father (even with "good reason") is often to find that, as an adult, he has rejected his own masculinity. He has rejected, in a manner of speaking, his father *within* himself. Through prayer, the son can be helped to accept his father, while at the same time he can reject and repudiate any of his father's sinful actions. In cases where the father has been particularly ignoble, hostile, or brutal, and the son has difficulty in separating the sin from the sinner, I lead him in a prayer of thanksgiving to God *for all He created the parent to be.* Then we go into a prayer where forgiveness is extended to the father for not becoming that completed person in Christ. The way is paved for God to touch and heal the father within the son, including the genetic inheritance from his father with all its potential in the very cells of the son's being.

God greatly blesses these prayers as I see many nearly ecstatic with relief after such simple prayers as these. For some, this is all that is needed to help them begin to integrate with their masculine side.

Closely related to the above is the matter of the childhood oath. In the frustration or pain of trying unsuccessfully to relate to a parent, a child may make a vow concerning this parent that will affect all his relationships in later life. Only a few weeks ago as I was sharing with medical professionals the problems which can arise out of childhood oaths, a physician's wife in the audience began to weep bitterly. She had struggled with a nearly total inability to communicate with her husband, her children, or her God. While I spoke, she remembered the strong oath she made as a child and carried out: a vow never again to speak freely to her father. Unless forced to say a word to him, she did not. In prayer she renounced this vow and received healing. Her mouth will no longer be stopped by a forgotten childhood vow. Such prayer is often called for in the case of persons suffering with homosexual gender confusion. They need help in order to renounce a childhood oath that has cut them off not only from a parent, but from that parent's gender identity within themselves. Truly, to fail to fully forgive a parent is to fail to be blessed within our very own spirits, souls, and bodies.

In the case of Judy, she needed to forgive her mother for being a very poor (even repulsive) feminine role model before she could go on to accept her own femininity. But her mother had to be forgiven for something else that was, in Judy's case, the chief cause behind her lesbian neurosis. An extremely unusual situation had developed between Judy and her mother, rare even for possessive and dominating mothers. From Judy's earliest childhood, her mother had systematically and exclusively demanded her daughter's full attention. She was especially keen on cutting her off from contacts with boys and men. The psychological effect of this was to make Judy woman-centered. There was simply no way the gender drive could develop. This possessiveness had been such an all-pervasive thing in Judy's life that she did not realize how perverse it was or that she needed to forgive her mother for it. She felt only guilt for putting half a continent between herself and her mother, and for not continuing to give the attention her mother demanded. The rage she felt toward her mother, though unacknowledged, wrought havoc in the depths of her soul.

Her mother, though Judy could not say it without profuse apologies for her, was like a vacuum cleaner, always ready to swoop her back up. Shuddering, she asked me why it affected her so terribly for her mother to say, as she often did, "My life revolves around you. You are my life." She immediately asked the Lord to forgive her for saying such a thing, and started telling me how basically good and well-meaning her mom was. She was amazed to hear me say that rather than apologizing for her mom, she must acknowledge the problem before the Lord and forgive her mother for her actions and words.

The Prayers and Understanding That Brought Judy's Healing

First I asked Judy if she was willing to repent of and absolutely turn from the lesbian lust. This she was only too willing to do, for, besides wanting to please God, she knew that overt lesbian behavior led only to more misery and did not solve her problem. Her prayer of repentance and the reception of forgiveness opened the way for her psychological healing.

She began to understand her gender confusion, and to see how her strong lesbian compulsions had come out of that. The following understanding made the symbolic nature of the problem altogether clear to her. I asked her what chiefly characterized each of the three women who "sparked" her. As she described

them, they were very like herself: successful, intellectually keen, and in possession of the power to initiate.
But there was one glaring exception. Each of the
women were intensely and wonderfully feminine.
Here we see the cannibal compulsion again. Judy's
strange and compelling drive to hold them and to be
held by them was merely a confusing signal of her
need to integrate with her own feminine side. She was
seeing *in them* her own alienated femininity; indeed,
she was projecting it onto them, and then attempting
to integrate with it in a physical manner. She was
amazed to see this, and her heart immediately recog-
nized the truth of it.

Besides needing to forgive her mother, Judy
needed prayer for the severing of her identity from
that of her mother's, along with prayer for a full inner
freedom from the bondages the maternal possessiveness and domination had wrought in her. The psychological need in such a case is no small one. As I write
in *The Broken Image:*

> To minister such a healing as this, we invoke the
> Presence of the Lord, asking for His power and
> love to come in and enable us to discern, and
> then to break, the oppressing bondages that have
> kept the person bound emotionally and spiritual-
> ly to another. There are different degrees to this
> problem, of course, but in some it is as though
> the soul is "possessed" by the soul of the mother.
> The prayer is much like one of exorcism, only it
> is for deliverance from the domination of the
> mother and her inroads into the very spirit and
> soul of the daughter. One said to me, "My moth-
> er has raped my mind." Another, "I can never

get away from the presence of my mother, even though I am hundreds of miles from her." It is truly a terrible bondage.

In a case such as this, false guilt will usually need to be dealt with first. Otherwise the woman may resist (albeit unconsciously) the healing and will rather berate and accuse herself for her problems with her mother. With her is the vague and irrational false guilt of never having been able to please her mother, never being able to meet her expectations, never being able to "love her enough." Pity and sadness for the emptiness in her mother's life will sometimes be paralyzing emotions within the false guilt. In completely disallowing her mother's psychological manipulation she will need to be released from fears that she is being unchristian and unloving. This psychological manipulation is, after all, what she has grown up to think of as "love." She must be assured that it is only after she has accepted her freedom (a full severing of her identity from that of her mother's) that she will be able to love and relate to her mother aright—as a whole, secure person. Until then, there is a part of her which is yet immature, yet under the law of her mother, yet subject to being manipulated. At last assured, she will be prepared to accept her freedom from the subjectivity that keeps her from maturing in some vital part of her personality, if not the whole of it.

In the prayer for such a one's release, I usually ask them to see Jesus with the eyes of their hearts, to see Him on the cross, there taking into Himself the very pain and bondage they are now struggling with, as well as any unforgiveness or sin within their hearts. I ask them to stretch out their hands to Him and see the pain and darkness flow into His outstretched, nailriven hands as I pray for the severance of their souls from the domination of their mother's. I often, without interrupting the rhythm of the prayer, softly ask them, "What are you seeing with the eyes of your heart?" And it is wonderful what they see as the darkness flows out of them and into Him. Often I will be seeing the same "picture" as the Holy Spirit leads the way.

Then, and I find this to be a very important step, I ask them to picture their mother. Because the Holy Spirit is in control and healing is so powerfully taking place, they will nearly always have a picture of her that is most revealing, one that will enable them to see her objectively for the first time, one that will better enable them to fully forgive her. Then I ask them to look and see if there are any bondages left between them. They will *see* it and *name* it. I then ask them, as though they had scissors in their hands, to cut through the bonds they see. The release that comes with this is often nothing short of phenomenal, and there are times when there are definite emotional and even physical reactions to the release. We will have seen these bonds sometimes as thick diseased umbilical cords, other times as threadlike ropes between the souls of the two, etc. When they are cut, we see a symbolic picture, one that is a true one, of the very deliverance that is taking place.[12]

It was precisely in this way that Judy and I prayed. As she forgave her mother, all the repressed anger and hostility she had been aware of began to well up and out of her heart and into our Lord's outstretched hands. From apologizing to Him for even acknowledging the fact that her mother *might* have a problem, she advanced to screaming at her mother: "Mother, every problem I've ever had goes back to you. You have messed me up so badly!" etc. This her heart had believed all along. Once the situation was consciously faced and admitted, Judy could be delivered of the repressed anger and could fully forgive her mother. Furthermore, she could, and did, take the fullest responsibility for her own actions, confessing them to the Lord. In prayer she named and cut the bondages between her and her mother, crying out, "I've got my mother's spirit in me, not Christ's." She "saw" a gray-brown spirit substance like a sticky cord coming from her mother and winding its way throughout her own body. This was, of course, the way her heart pictured the diseased form of mother-love she had known. I continued to pray for her until she saw all this substance flow from her into the cruci-fied body of our Lord. I then prayed for the love and light of Christ to enter in and fill all those spaces where the bondage had been.

After this separation of her identity from that of her mother, there was yet another very important healing needed. I asked the Lord to enter into her and to find and affirm the beautiful *woman* within. We continued to pray, with laying on of hands, as Jesus touched and healed her in her femininity. There was no way, of course, that she could release faith for this, but I, as minister, could. Last, I prayed for the gift of chastity and celibacy for her until such time as she married—a prayer that surprised her. I explained that I did this because a repressed gender drive, when released, has a way of making up for lost time. That very weekend she phoned me, amazed at herself. In a business meeting with a young widower, a Christian man, she experienced for the first time the feminine gender drive. "I've waited a lifetime for this. I sure am glad you prayed for the gift of chastity!" This young woman is wonderfully whole today, and her very physical appearance reflects the balance of the masculine and the feminine in her life.

Masculine and Feminine

Masculine and feminine can be understood only in terms of each other; basically they are opposite and complementary qualities, similar to darkness and light. It is very hard to understand darkness except in terms of light, and light except in terms of darkness. They are two extremes on a continuum. The masculine and the feminine within man and within woman, by whatever name they are called, or by whatever they are understood to be, seek recognition, affirmation, and their proper balance. Much that is called emotional illness or instability today (as I continually discover in prayer and counselling sessions) is merely the masculine and/or the feminine unaffirmed and out of balance within the personality. *Merely* is always, as C. S. Lewis has said, a dangerous word, and it surely is in this case if one does not recognize the potentially fatal blow an imbalance of the masculine and the feminine can wield, whether to the health of an individual, a society, or an entire civilization.

The Harrowing of Hell

Over my desk hangs an icon depicting the time between Christ's crucifixion and resurrection. It is entitled "The Harrowing of Hell." In it, Christ has descended into hell and stands solidly over Satan, who is defeated on his own territory and is securely bound. Christ, the Victor, has thrust down strong arms to Adam and Eve, and they are firmly in His grasp. He is pulling them up from the regions of the damned.

So it is in the ministry of inner healing. Our Lord descends into the subconscious hells of those who choose to give themselves to Him but nevertheless are trapped by their past (the consequence of their own sins and their grievous reactions to the sins of others). And He harrows their individual hells. He unbinds them, cleanses them, and raises them up. Through us, as we learn to pray, He reaps "the harvest that is produced by distress and conviction of sin."

Notes

1. Leanne Payne, *The Broken Image: Restoring Personal Wholeness Through Healing Prayer* (Westchester, Ill.: Crossway Books, 1981), p. 138.
2. *Ibid.*, pp. 46-48.
3. *Ibid.*, pp. 66-73.
4. For discussion on all these views, see Ruth Tiffany Barnhouse, *Homosexuality: A Symbolic Confusion* (New York: The Seabury Press, 1977). That book provides concise and comprehensive insight, as well as responsible analyses of factors outside the scientific and medical that are contributing to the current demands to accept homosexuality as normal, therefore psychologically healthy and moral. As a scholar and researcher, she exposes inadequate arguments along with their faulty presuppositions and statistical data, and thereby takes the spurious scientific mask off much of the current jargon. In addition, she puts the whole problem in its historical perspective, and as both practicing psychiatrist and theologian, she recognizes when the various issues are outside their proper scientific and/or moral domain.
5. Oswald Chambers, *My Utmost for His Highest* (New York: Dodd, Mead, and Co., n.d.), October 16 reading.
6. Agnes Sanford, *The Healing Gifts of the Spirit* (Philadelphia: J. B. Lippincott, n.d.), pp. 126, 127.
7. C. S. Lewis, *The Problem of Pain* (New York: Macmillan, 1962), p. 61.

8. Leanne Payne, *Real Presence: The Holy Spirit in the Works of C. S. Lewis* (Westchester, Ill.: Crossway Books, 1979), pp. 147, 148.

9. C. S. Lewis, *Surprised by Joy* (New York: Harcourt Brace Jovanovich, 1966), p. 219.

10. For more understanding of this, see Payne, *Real Presence*, Chapters 11 and 12 on "The Whole Imagination" and *The Broken Image*, Chapter 6, "Listening for the Healing Word."

11. Payne, *The Broken Image*, pp. 49-52, 54-58.

12. *Ibid.*, pp. 104-106.